You
can create a
Killer
SCIENCE FAIR
Project!

Written by Kris Hirschmann

Designed by Nancy Panaccione

Cover design by Bill Henderson

Selected illustrations by Joshua & Jacob Panaccione

an imprint of
SCHOLASTIC
www.scholastic.com

Published by Tangerine Press, an imprint of Scholastic Inc.;

557 Broadway; New York, NY 10012

10 9 8 7 6 5 4 3 2 1

ISBN: 978-0-545-27032-8

Printed and bound in Heshan, China

What's in Here For You

Table of Contents:

Section I: Finding an Idea

Big Ideas

Section II: Research & Hypothesis

Section III: Design Your Experiment

Section IV: Data and Conclusions

Section V: Putting It All Together

A Science Fair? Great Idea!

If you're reading this book, there's probably a science fair in your future. Maybe you have decided to enter the fair on your own. Or maybe your teacher is making you do it. Either way, there's a bunch of work to do—and it's **all up to you.**

Does that idea scare you? It shouldn't. Sure, science fair projects are a big deal. But here's the thing: **You don't have to be a genius to pull off a killer project**. You just have to take things step by step. Tackle a chunk today, a chunk tomorrow, a chunk next week, and so on. You'll have a huge, impressive pile of chunks—also known as a **finished science fair project**—before you know it!

Don't Blow the Chunks

So, let's talk a little bit more about those chunks. They're the key to the whole thing. Get them right, and you get the project right. Get them wrong, and you could be looking at a big, fat mess. Obviously, you can't afford to blow the chunks.

That's where this book comes in. Think of it as your science fair chunktionary. We're going to break things down into understandable, easy-to-manage pieces. You're going to assemble the pieces into a project.

Easy, peasy, one-two-threesie.

Sneak Preview

The science fair process has five **BIG** chunks. This book breaks each **BIG** chunk into several **smaller** ones. Use the tabs to find the topics you need.

Part I: **Finding an Idea** (and making it cool)

Part II: **Research and Hypothesis** (also known as learning and guessing)

Part III: **Designing Your Experiment** (or, figuring out what to do)

Part IV: **Data and Conclusions** (or, crunching numbers and getting results)

Part V: **Pulling It All Together** (preparing for science fair day)

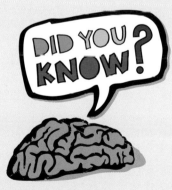

DID YOU KNOW?

Science fairs first became popular in the 1950s. Today, an estimated 75,000 American students enter science fairs each year.

What Are You Getting Yourself Into?

Okay, confession time. When we used the phrase **easy, peasy, one-two-threesie** on the previous page, we might have ignored one tiny fact. Science fairs aren't all rainbows, butterflies, and peel-me-a-grape simple. **The truth is:**

Science fair projects can be a lot of work.

Let's be clear on what we mean here. We are **not** saying that a science fair project has to be hard, or complicated, or confusing. **It does not.** A science fair project **does**, however, require focus and organization. It also takes time—and that's where the "lot of work" sometimes comes in.

So, why do it? Because the rewards are huge, that's why!

Studies show that science fairs can:

✓ **Boost your thinking skills**

✓ **Build your self-confidence**

✓ **Increase your organization level**

✓ **Teach you how to set goals**

✓ **Make you more responsible**

✓ **Impress your peers and teachers**

And that's just the beginning. Science fairs can also make you a better reader, writer, and speaker. They give you the chance to draw pictures, snap photos, build things, meet people, or do just about anything else you enjoy. They may even let you win stuff. **All of which means:**

Science fair projects can be a lot of fun.

Make sure your project is fun. Start by adopting a good attitude. Then, pick a topic you'll enjoy and allow plenty of time to get the work done. These simple steps will put you on a guaranteed path to science fair success.

LOVE A-FAIR

Science fairs are great places to make new friends who share your interests. "I like meeting other kids who are also passionate about science," says one frequent science fair participant.

About 400 students enter a science fair called the Intel Science Talent Search each year. This competition awards $100,000 for first place, $75,000 for second place, and $50,000 for third place. Cha-ching!

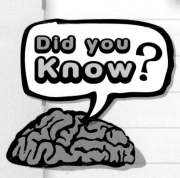
Did you Know?

9

The Scientific Method

So, you have a lot of work to do, and you're wondering where to start.

How should you tackle the science fair challenge?

Well, we have some good news about that. **You don't need to reinvent the wheel here.** There's a science fair road map that lays out each and every step you need to take, from start to finish. This map is called the **scientific method**.

"Scientific method." That sounds awfully **official**. Maybe even a little **intimidating**. But it's very, very simple. It's just a way to break the experimental process into steps. **Six of them**, actually.

Simply put, they are:

1 Ask a question. Who, What, When, Where, Why, How, Which? Observe something—**anything**—and apply these words. **You're on your way!**

2 Research the question. Research gives you information about your question. It also shows you what other scientists have done. This keeps you from repeating old mistakes.

3 Form a hypothesis. This is an educated guess about the answer to your question. (We'll talk more about the hypothesis on PP. 40-41.)

4 Do an experiment to test your hypothesis. This is the biggie. The success of your science fair project hinges on it.

5 Analyze your data and draw a conclusion. What did your experiment prove? This is your chance to find out.

6 Present your results. Tell the world what you know. Then, take a bow!

Why Use the Method?

The scientific method isn't just for kids like you. Professional scientists use it, too. They know these steps are incredibly useful. They offer a tried-and-true way to answer scientific questions.

Pretty helpful, eh? Yeah, we think so, too. Tell you what: We'll walk you through the process. You follow along. You'll be rolling in **no time at all**!

Same Old, Same Old

One of the great benefits of the scientific method is that it's **repeatable**. The **same** experiment done with the **same** steps under the **same** circumstances should yield the **same** results. This means that scientists can **check up on each other**—and they do it all the time!

Tick...Tick...Tick...

Hello again! Glad to see you're still with us. You must be really serious about this science fair thing. So, great. **Let's get started.**

"What??" you may be saying. *"Right now?"*

Yes. Now. Your science fair may be months away. That's, like, eons, right? Maybe so. But no matter how much time you have, **the countdown clock is already ticking**. You have a lot of stuff to do. The sooner you figure out what that stuff is, the better off you'll be.

That's where a project timeline comes in handy. The timeline is not exactly a schedule. It is more like an overview or a "guesstimate" of roughly how long your project will take. This reveals your last-chance, drop-dead, no-kidding start date—and that's definitely a good thing to know! **No more waiting until the night before!**

SCHOOL'S OUT

Check for holidays when planning your project. If you really want to work over spring break, that's fine. If not, don't forget to add those days onto your timeline.

Sample Timeline

Here's what a timeline looks like. The student who created this timeline will need at least 60 days, or two months, to complete the project. In other words: If the science fair is on April 30, she needs to start working by March 1. No **ifs, ands,** or **buts** about it.

Timeline Task	Days Needed
Choose my topic	3
Do research/form hypothesis	7
Design my experiment	7
Buy or order equipment	6
Set up my experiment	3
Do my experiment	21
Draw conclusions	2
Write research report	7
Create display	4
TOTAL	**60**

Helpful Hint

The actual experiment is the most flexible part of your timeline. Choose a short experiment if your science fair is coming up soon. Choose a longer experiment if you have plenty of time.

--- fig A.

strand

Your timeline might be very different from this one. Maybe you think you can choose a topic in one day. Or maybe you want extra time to write your report, or maybe your teacher has given you a timeline. Consider your own strengths and needs before making a timeline for **your** project.

Doing Things by the Book

See this box over here? Take a good look, because it's important.

Take Note:

Turn to P. 1 of your logbook. Write down a timeline for your project.

Take Note! Boxes pop up all over this book. They tell you how and when to use your handy-dandy **project log.** Didn't see the log? Check inside the back cover of this book. **Yeah, there it is.**

The project log is going to help you **a lot** as you prepare for your science fair. It gives you a place to plan, to scribble ideas, to record data, to crunch numbers, and much more. It keeps all of these notes in one easy-to-find place. It also acts as a record of your thoughts and findings. On science fair day, the judges will want to see the logbook. So, **use it** and **don't lose it**. From now on, we're going to be doing things strictly by the book. **Yes, this one!**

P.S. Did you actually follow the instructions in the *Take Note!* box? Or did you just look at them? Come on, scientist. Do it now.

Finding an Idea

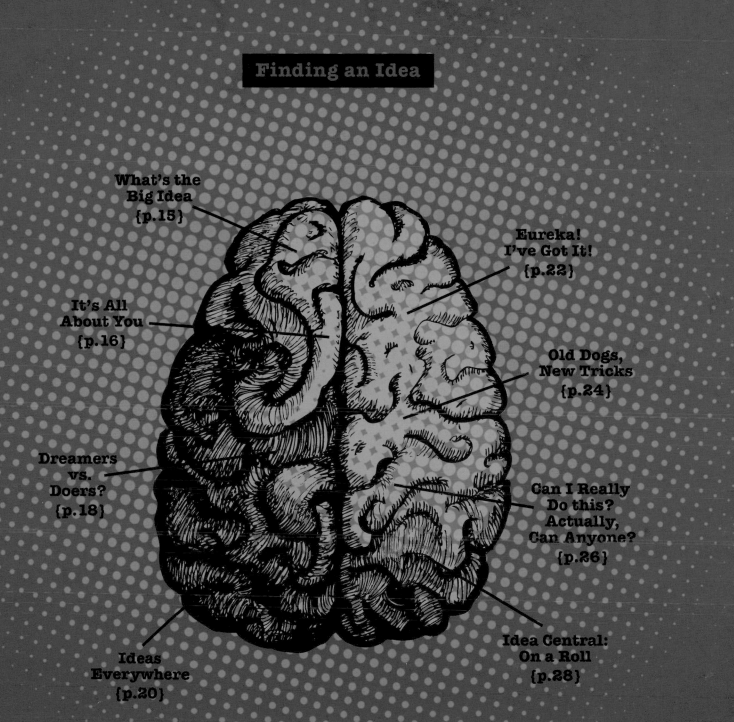

What's the
Big Idea
{p.15}

It's All
About You
{p.16}

Dreamers
vs.
Doers?
{p.18}

Ideas
Everywhere
{p.20}

Eureka!
I've Got It!
{p.22}

Old Dogs,
New Tricks
{p.24}

Can I Really
Do this?
Actually,
Can Anyone?
{p.26}

Idea Central:
On a Roll
{p.28}

What's the Big Idea?

So, you're **committed**, you're **primed**, you're **pumped**.

You're ready to get started on your science fair project.

There's just one teensy-weensy problem:

You're drawing a big, fat blank when it comes to project (ideas).

This might seem like a major obstacle. But guess what? It isn't. The world is full of spectacular science topics. You just need to know **how** and **where** to look for them. Countless science fair participants before you have figured it out. With the help of this section, **you're going to do it**, too. Get ready to go from totally clueless… to totally clued-in!

Written in Ink

Use a pen when writing in your logbook. Judges don't like pencil writing. It's too easy to erase or change.

It's All About You

Your first clue isn't going to come from a book, or a magazine, or a website (although we'll get to those things later). It's going to come from **you**.

By this, we mean that your topic needs to be near and dear to your heart. In other words, you should **like** it. Heck, you should **love** it. Why? Because as you already know, this project is going to take a lot of work. You'll have more fun if you're truly curious about your topic. You'll do a better job, too.

So, let's start with a quickie brainstorming session. Think about past assignments and subjects you liked. ("Dissecting the frog was **totally sick**." "That book about flesh-eating plants was **wicked cool**.") Write down everything that pops into your head. This list will be your starting point. It will help you to create a workable science fair project.

Love

Using Your Resources

A participant at a recent science fair was happy to use his family's resources. "I am the son of a potato farmer. I love learning all about how the machinery works and how the plants grow," he said on his application.

Hook Me Up

Your interests aren't the only things you should list. You need to include your **resources**, too. Resources are things or knowledge you already have, or that you can get easily.

A resource might be:

 **A hobby.** Many hobbies involve special skills and equipment. Think about ways to turn your hobby into a science fair project.

Specialty stuff. Does your uncle run a garden shop? If so, maybe you can get all the **free plants** you want. Is your mom an electrician? She's probably loaded with wire, switches, and other **cool equipment**. You can use these things in your project.

A smart person. Maybe your accountant dad is, like, a human calculator. Or maybe your cousin is an expert bird-watcher. Use these skills to your advantage.

Remember:

When it comes to resources, don't be afraid to pick a few brains. Most people are show-offs. They want a chance to display their expertise. Which means they'll probably be thrilled to help you. And their help might just make you—and your project—stand out from the crowd.

Take Note: Turn to P. 2 of your logbook. Make a list of your burning interests and special resources.

Dreamers vs. Doers?

Great job on the brainstorming! You've identified your interests and resources. You're starting to have a clue. Now let's take it one step further. It's time to figure out what **type of project** you'd like to do.

There are two main types of science fair projects:

INVESTIGATIONS

In an investigation, you'll come up with a question. You'll learn as much as you can about it. Then, you'll design and run an experiment that answers the question.

INVENTIONS

In an invention project, you'll identify a real-world problem. You'll invent a gadget to solve that problem. Then, you'll test the invention to see how well it works.

Which type of project is right for you? It depends. Do you love reading and thinking? Does the idea of running an experiment excite you? **You might want to try an investigation.** Are you a good problem solver? Do you love to work with your hands? **An invention project might be right up your alley.**

Some science fairs are for inventions only. These fairs are sometimes called "invention conventions."

DID YOU KNOW?

No Easy Way Out

At this point, you may be wondering which type of project is simpler. Maybe you're thinking you'll just choose the easier one. **Don't bother.** Investigations and inventions are equally challenging. In fact, they have a lot in common.

No matter what, you're gonna be:

- ✓ **Asking questions**
- ✓ **Researching**
- ✓ **Planning**
- ✓ **Scheduling**
- ✓ **Assembling materials**
- ✓ **Recording data**
- ✓ **Creating a science fair display**

Yep, you're going to be busy either way. So, **embrace it; accept it; be it.** Put the word "easy" out of your mind. Then, pick the type of project that suits your skills and personality. Once you do, go ahead and flip the page. We're about to look a little more closely at your actual science fair topic.

The "Zzzz" Factor

Certain types of projects are notorious snoozers. They've been putting science fair judges to sleep for decades. Make absolutely, positively, 100% sure you have something original to say before tackling these ho-hum classics.

- ○ **Models:** Of DNA, buildings, the solar system, human organs, and so on.

- ○ **Displays:** Of your rock collection, fall leaves from your backyard, seashells, etc.

- ○ **Surveys:** Of hygiene habits, weeds on the P.E. field, dogs vs. cats, yada yada yada.

Ideas Everywhere

By now, you have a few vague ideas about your science fair project. That's good…but it's not good enough. **"Vague"** isn't going to cut it. You need to find something specific that **fascinates** you. And you need it **pronto**!

So, where are you going to find it? Well, anywhere, really. There are endless sources of ideas. **Here are the most popular ones.**

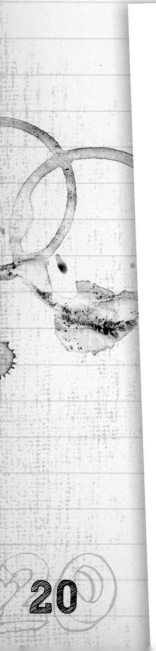

The library. Your school or local library is a science fair bonanza. You can browse books on science topics. (In the Dewey Decimal System, they're filed in the 500s.) You can look at magazines such as **National Geographic**, **Popular Science**, **Discover**, and many more. Newspaper articles can also give you science-related ideas. Ask a librarian for suggestions.

The Internet. There's enough science info on the Internet to keep you reading 24/7 for 176,892 years. Okay, we made that up. But seriously, there's a LOT of stuff. Use a search engine like Google (www.google.com) or Yahoo (www.yahoo.com) to look up anything your little heart desires.

Your TV. Yes, watching TV can be good for you! Check out the shows on Discovery, the Science Channel, Animal Planet, and other science-oriented channels. They're guaranteed to fan your science fair flame.

Information Overload

If you have even one curious bone in your body, you're not going to have any trouble finding ideas. In fact, you might have the opposite problem. **It might be hard to narrow things down.**

Focus is the key to avoiding this problem. **Remember** your main interests. **Remember** your resources. **Remember** your project type. Then **skip** subjects that don't fit into all three categories. Sure, a random article may catch your eye. But don't get bogged down. Fish for ideas now; read for fun later. It's a winning strategy for any aspiring scientist.

Check it out:

We can't list every great website. But we're too nice to leave you high and dry. Here are a few cool sites to browse. Make sure you have a parent's permission before going on the Internet.

Discovery Channel (dsc.discovery.com)

Exploratorium (www.exploratorium.com)

Fact Monster (www.factmonster.com)

How Stuff Works: Science (science.howstuffworks.com)

NASA (www.nasa.gov)

Yahoo! Kids: Science (kids.yahoo.com/science)

Take Note:

Turn to P. 3 of your logbook. Jot down any interesting ideas you come across in your reading.

Eureka! I've Got It!

You've read, you've browsed, you've watched TV.

And the effort has paid off! Your logbook is bulging with incredible ideas. You're excited about each and every one of them.

Now it's time to get more specific. You need to choose your **very favorite idea**—the one that really **knocks your socks off**. You're going to boil it down to a single question. This question will be your **topic**.

Imagine a trumpet fanfare here

Da-da-da-DA!
THE TOPIC
IS A
BIG DEAL.

Did we get your attention? Good, because this concept is important.

Your topic is like a springboard. It's the starting point for the next few weeks or months of your life. So, choose wisely. Make sure your topic is something you can live with and, yes, even **love!**

Boiling It Down

Let's talk for a moment about **interests vs. ideas vs. topics**.

An **interest** may be very broad. An **idea** is narrower. A **topic** zooms in on one small aspect of your idea. Check out the difference in the examples below.

Interest: Light and heat

Idea: It's cool that different colors absorb different amounts of heat.

Topic: Which popsicle melts fastest in sunlight: red, orange, or purple?

Interest: Model cars

Idea: I want my models to go faster!

Topic: Which lubricant works best on model car wheels?

Interest: Sports

Idea: Some foods and drinks might make me better at sports.

Topic: Do energy drinks improve reaction time?

A Mythbusters Moment

The scientists on the Discovery Channel's "Mythbusters" have the same topic for every project: **"Is (insert myth here) really true?"** This simple question has launched hundreds of fascinating experiments for the "Mythbusters" crew.

Time to try it yourself!

Think about your own interests and ideas. How could you turn them into science fair topics?

Take Note:

Turn to P. 4 of your logbook. List some possible science fair topics.

Old Dogs, New Tricks

Perhaps you're a bit confused at this point. "Why do I have to work **SO HARD** on my topic?" you might be thinking. "There are **books** full of experiments. There are **lists** on the Internet. I can choose from **them**."

You're right. You can. But you shouldn't.

Why not? There are a couple of good reasons. **First of all, judges and teachers didn't just fall off the turnip truck.** They'll be able to tell if you pulled your project straight out of a book. There's nothing actually **wrong** with that; you won't get in trouble or anything. But you won't get a top score on your project, either.

The second reason is, shall we say, **loftier**. It has to do with you personally. You're supposed to be honing your science skills here. You can't do that if you're copying someone else's work. Right? **So don't.**

A New Twist

That's not to say that you can **never** use project lists. They can be very helpful, especially if you've never done a science fair before. But they are best used for **inspiration**, not **instruction**. In other words: Take an old idea and put a new twist on it. **Voilà!** Originality rocks!

Check it out!

We've given a classic topic a facelift. See how easy it is? **You can do it, too!**

`CLASSIC TOPIC:` **Do plants grow better with music?**

In the classic version, bean plants are grown with or without music playing in the background. The scientist figures out if one method works better.

`NEW+IMPROVED:` **Do plants have musical taste?**

This is much more interesting! You could choose several different types of seeds. Let's say beans, radishes, and flowers. You'd grow one bean, one radish, and one flower with rock music. You'd grow another batch with country music and maybe one with classical. You would check for differences in the seeds' responses.

Helpful Hint

Don't be afraid to ask for advice, if you need it. You can be original without flying totally solo.

Science Everywhere

"Science is everywhere! It's what we breathe, what we can touch, hear, and see. It's also everything beyond our planet, beyond what we know. That's really amazing," says a 5th-grade science fair participant.

Can I Really Do This?
Actually, Can Anyone?

Way to go! You've settled on a topic. Before you make it official, though, you have one last thing to do. You need to **validate your topic**.

"Validate" is a fancy word for "foolproof."

It basically means **you gotta run that idea through the ringer.**

You need to **poke it** and **prod it** and see if it has any weak spots.

Why? Because if you don't, you might find yourself stuck with an impossible project. Is that what you want? Nope, we didn't think so.

Did You Know?
When phrased as a question, the science fair topic is also called the **problem.**

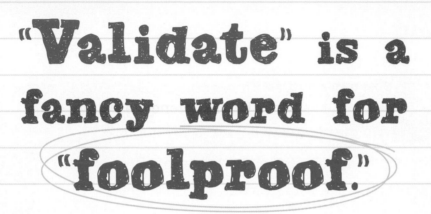

Take Note:

Turn to P. 5 of your logbook. Fill out the checklist to validate your topic.

Validating a topic isn't tricky. You just have to ask the right questions.

This list will help you to do it. If any "**Nos**" pop up, it's time to tweak. When you can say "**Yes**" to everything, you're in business. **Congratulations!**

Think about your:	Ask these questions:
Question:	Does my topic have a specific answer or solution? Is there a reasonable way to find that answer or solution?
Time:	Do I have enough time? Can I finish the work before science fair day?
Materials:	Can I get or make the materials I need? Can I afford them?
Safety:	Is my project safe? Is it ethical?
Level:	Do I really understand the topic? Can I find resources that aren't too advanced?
Originality:	Is my topic interesting or original in some way? Will anyone care?
Interest:	Am I truly interested in this topic?

No, No, No, and No

These topics are not valid. Can you guess why?

A. The Truth Is Out There: All About the Solar System

B. Growing an Oak: From Acorn to Tree

C. Are Diamonds Really Forever?: Crushing Gemstones

D. Do Bats Really Carry Rabies?: Testing Different Species

Answers:

A. How in the world would you answer this? **B.** This will take way, way, way too long. **C.** A bit pricey, don't you think? **D.** Neither safe nor ethical. 'Nuff said.

On a Roll

With a little creativity, you can turn any boring question into an interesting experiment. Here's an example.

The Idea:

Rafe is picky about his toilet paper. **Picky, picky, picky**. He wonders if other people feel the same way. For his science fair project, he thinks he might log people's TP preferences.

The Problem:

Asking people what they think isn't good enough. It's just a survey. Rafe needs to turn his survey into an investigation.

The Solution:

Rafe does his survey. Then, with the principal's permission, he stocks different school bathroom stalls with different types of TP. He tracks toilet paper consumption in each stall to see if the students' preferences match their behavior. He has found an experiment that backs up his survey. **Mission accomplished!**

Things to Think About:

 Should the stall doors be labeled with the names of their TP for easy ID?

 How much TP will I need? (A lot, probably.)

How's going to restock the stalls? How can I make sure it's done promptly?

 How can I make sure that all students have equal access to all types of TP?

Should I shift things around each day, so different types of TP appear in different stalls?

 Other issues (come up with your own): _____

Research & Hypothesis

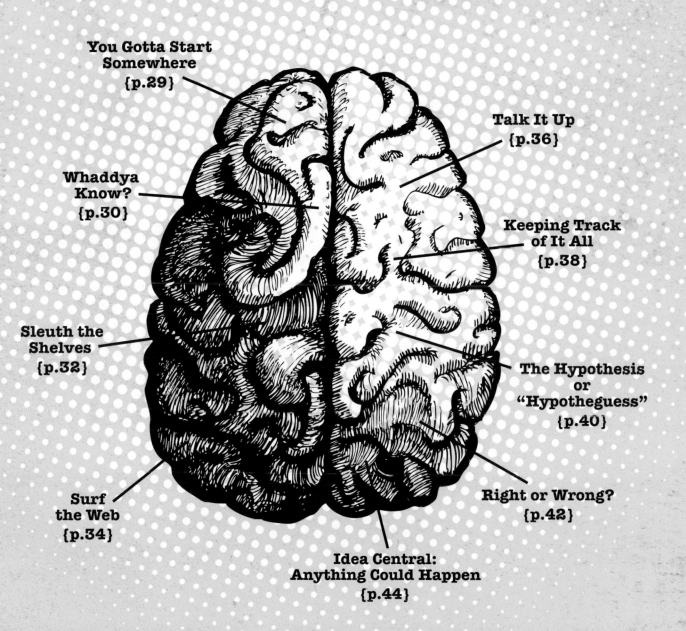

You Gotta Start
Somewhere
{p.29}

Talk It Up
{p.36}

Whaddya
Know?
{p.30}

Keeping Track
of It All
{p.38}

Sleuth the
Shelves
{p.32}

The Hypothesis
or
"Hypotheguess"
{p.40}

Surf
the Web
{p.34}

Right or Wrong?
{p.42}

Idea Central:
Anything Could Happen
{p.44}

Research & Hypothesis

You Gotta Start Somewhere

You've chosen your science fair topic. **You rock!** But hold that sigh of relief. The science jam session is far from over.

You still have a lot of (work) to do.

So, what happens next? Research, that's what! You need to become an expert in your science fair field. This is going to take a little **reading**, a little **web-surfing**, a little **talking**, a little **thinking**. Or maybe a lot of those things. **It depends on your topic.**

Either way, we've got you covered. This section will point you in the right direction for research success. It will also help you to form a hypothesis.

start

Hypothe-WHAT?
Read on to find out!

Anything Could Happen

The null hypothesis comes in very handy when you have no idea what your results will be. Like, for instance, in the experiment below.

The Idea:

Georgia hates sugar substitutes. Yet some people swear these substances taste exactly like sugar. Georgia is curious about this. She decides to find out if artificial sweeteners can fool the ultimate sugar experts: **ants**. She plans to put out every sweetener she can find and see which ones the ants eat.

The Problem:

Georgia does a lot of research. But she can't find any information on her topic. She **thinks** the ants will respond differently to different sweeteners, but she isn't sure. So she doesn't know what her hypothesis should be.

The Solution:

Georgia uses the null hypothesis: **Ants will respond equally to natural and artificial sweeteners.** She's excited about proving herself wrong—and explaining why later.

Things to Think About:

 How will I measure the ants' response?

 If the ants do show a clear preference for one substance, how will I explain it? Are there experts I can talk to?

Do I know where to find an ant colony?
If so, am I sure that these particular ants like sugar?

 Ants are living creatures.
Is it ethical to use them in my project?

Other issues (come up with your own)

_____

Design Your Experiment

Success by Design

You are doing a **fantastic** job! So far, you've nailed down your topic. You've done your research. You've formed your hypothesis. **Feels good, doesn't it?**

And it's about to feel even better. In this section, you're going to make use of your newfound knowledge. You're going to **twist** it and **turn** it and **shape** it.

You're going to mold it into an actual experiment.

There's a lot of stuff to learn along the way. But never fear.

We've got you covered. Just stick with us and listen up.

> We'll give you the tools to bring your experiment to life.

What You Change... and What You Don't

So, you have your hypothesis. Now you need to prove (or disprove) it. To do this, you'll be running some tests. But you have to figure out exactly what you're testing first.

A well-designed experiment tests a single thing. The thing you're testing is called the **independent variable**. You could also call it **"the thing that changes."** You'll change the independent variable and see what happens as a result.

This result has a name, too. It's called the **dependent variable**. It is called this because it **depends on** the independent variable. You make a change; something happens. **It's that simple**.

An Example

We're bored of squirrels. Let's choose a new example for a new section. Like...hmmm...**rotting teeth**.

Here's the idea. Your mom is always telling you that sugary drinks will rot your teeth. It's, like, so annoying. But you wonder if maybe, possibly, she could be right. You've come up with **your problem: Do sugary drinks really rot your teeth**? You're reluctantly going to side with your mom on this one, so your **hypothesis is: Sugary drinks will cause human teeth to decay.**

To prove this hypothesis, you'll have to expose some old baby teeth to sugary drinks. You'd like to test three liquids: juice, sports drink, and soda. In other words, **the type of drink will change**. Which means it is your **independent variable**. Everything else should stay the same.

Things that would stay the same include:

⇨ The approximate size of the teeth

⇨ The temperature of the drinks

⇨ The location of the experiments

⇨ The containers used

⇨ The amount of drink in each container

⇨ The time the teeth spend in each liquid

What Happens?

So, you set up three cups. You fill the cups with your three drinks. Then, you drop a tooth into each cup. After a couple of days you see that the teeth are, indeed, rotting.

See how that works? You manipulated a condition and something changed as a result. **Supereasy**, and yet **superscientific**. You're on your way to resultsville.

A Few More Examples

You need to be really clear on this independent vs. dependent thing. Check out a few more examples below.

Independent:
Items in a food mixture

Dependent:
Which items squirrels choose most

Independent:
Amount of water given

Dependent:
How quickly plants grow

Independent:
Color of ice pop

Dependent:
Speed of melting in sunlight

```
Helpful Hint
The teeth-in-sugar experiment has been done a LOT. We're using
it because it's easy to explain. But you should come up with a
new twist if you want to use this experiment yourself.
```

Keeping It Under Control

Let's go back to our tooth example. Remember, you put the teeth into juice, sports drink, and soda. The teeth started to rot. You're pretty sure your mom is right. Sugar really does rot your teeth.

But **hold your horses, bucko.** How do you know sugar is rotting those teeth? Maybe **any** liquid rots teeth. Maybe **sunlight** is doing it. Maybe **the tooth fairy's evil, destructive twin** is messing with your mind.

Do you see what we mean? Yes, you're getting results. But thousands of things could have caused them. Which means you haven't really learned a thing.

This is where something called a **control** comes in handy. **A control is an experimental trial in which nothing is manipulated.** Put another way: That independent variable? You're going to leave it alone. **Hands off.**

Control Issues

How can we apply this to our tooth experiment? **Easy.** Soak one tooth in a drink with no sugar whatsoever. (Water, anyone?) **Leave all other experimental conditions the same.**

So, now you have four cups.

Imagine that the sugary-drink teeth rot. The water tooth doesn't.

What have you learned?

☑ **1.** Teeth do not rot in water.

☑ **2.** Teeth do rot in sugary drinks.

☑ **3.** The **only** difference between the trials was the amount of sugar in the liquid.

☑ **4.** Therefore, sugar probably caused the teeth to rot.

See how that works? Without a control, you can't be confident about your results. With a control, you can be pretty darn sure you're right. So, use controls in your experiment. You'll get answers that you—**and the judges**—can believe in.

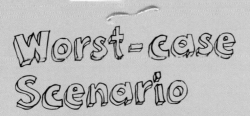
Worst-case Scenario

In our example, what if the fourth tooth did rot in water? Then you'd know that something other than sugar rotted the teeth. This would mean your hypothesis was wrong. Time to start looking for that **disgruntled fairy**.

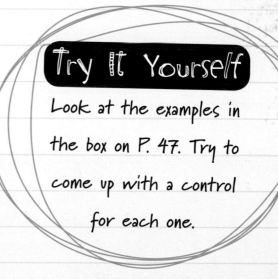
Try It Yourself
Look at the examples in the box on P. 47. Try to come up with a control for each one.

But What If I'm Building Something?

The word "experiment" has popped up an awful lot of times in the last few pages. But what if you aren't planning to do an investigation? What if you're **building** something? Are you exempt from all this variable-control-procedure stuff?

Here's the problem with that. It isn't enough to just invent something. You have to invent something that **works**, or at least has a **hope of working**. And to prove that your invention works, what are you going to do?

That's right. You're going to experiment with it. You saw that one coming a mile away, didn't you?

Love the Process

In his science fair bio, a 14-year-old boy talks about inventions. "I LOVE building things. To be able to take an idea from paper and fabricate it into a 3-D working object is fantastic," he says.

An Example

Here's a simple example. Imagine you're **way** into model cars. For your science fair project, you decide to add solar panels to your favorite model.

Okay, that's a start. But you can't just stick a solar panel on a car. Your contraption has to actually work.

Car + Sunlight = zoom zoom.

You'll need to run tests to prove that this equation is true.

And then there's the **blue-ribbon factor**. For a higher score on your project, you might want to check a few more things. Like your car's maximum speed, or its performance in early-morning sunlight vs. noon sunlight, or whether it holds a charge after it is brought indoors, or whatever interests you most. And all those questions can be answered by what? Say it with us: **experimenting**.

You know the drill by now. Form a hypothesis. Design an experiment. Do the experiment. Show the judges why your invention is the most incredible, amazing, awesome thing in the room...**and learn a little science while you're at it.**

Try, Try Again

Successful inventors tweak their designs again and again until they get the results they want. Orville and Wilbur Wright, the brothers who built the world's first airplane, tested more than 200 wing and airframe designs before they found one that worked.

K.I.S.S.
(Keep It Simple, Scientist)

There's something we want to discuss in a bit more detail. On the last page, we talked about ways to get a higher score on your project. **We suggested beefing up your experiment to impress the judges.**

That's all fine and dandy. Judges do like to see a little heavy lifting. But…and this is a big "but"…**that's not what they like most**.

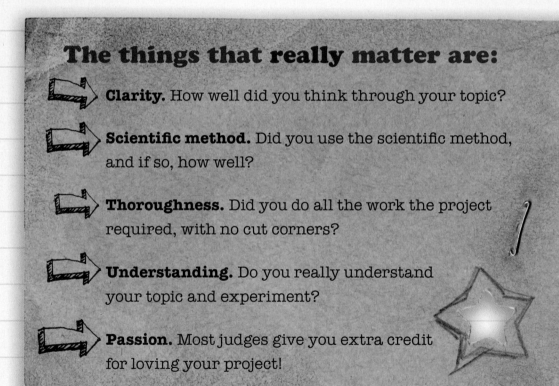

The things that really matter are:

➡️ **Clarity.** How well did you think through your topic?

➡️ **Scientific method.** Did you use the scientific method, and if so, how well?

➡️ **Thoroughness.** Did you do all the work the project required, with no cut corners?

➡️ **Understanding.** Do you really understand your topic and experiment?

➡️ **Passion.** Most judges give you extra credit for loving your project!

To nail all of these points, follow the **K.I.S.S.** rule: **Keep It Simple, Scientist**. It's better to do a fantastic job on a simple project than a so-so job on a tricky one. **Remember this fact when designing your experiment.**

Simple Is Good

Our tooth experiment is simple. You're putting teeth into liquids. You're letting them soak for a few days. Then you're taking them out and observing them. **You can handle that.** In fact, **it would probably be hard to mess it up**.

But what if you decide to make things a little more complicated? Let's say you want to see if shark teeth rot in sugar, too. You'd like to compare them to human teeth. Interesting? Sure. However, you've just doubled your work. Which doubles your chance of making a mistake. You've also added a whole new angle to your research, which means you have a LOT more explaining to do.

See how quickly things can spiral out of control? Don't let this happen to you. Choose a simple question, and then design a simple experiment to answer it. You'll be happier in the long run. And you'll do just fine in the science fair, too. **That's a promise.**

SIMPLE VS. EASY

When it comes to science fair projects, there is a difference between **simple** and **easy**. Simple means straightforward and uncomplicated. **That's fine.** Easy means below your abilities and, let's face it, a little bit babyish. **That's not so fine.** The goal is to challenge yourself while keeping things manageable. Focus on this goal as you plan your experiment.

Did you Know?

Yes-or-no hypotheses are about as simple as it gets. No matter how you test 'em, you only have two possible results!

What's the Procedure?

You now know **what** you're testing, and you have a few clues about **how** to test it. Your experiment is starting to take shape.

This means it's time to take the ⟨plunge.⟩

That's right: You're going to make a **commitment**. (Eek!) You're going to **think through** your experiment-to-be, from start to finish. You're going to **write down** every single step you need to take. When the time comes, you're going to **follow those steps** until your experiment is complete.

Your step-by-step plan is called your **procedure**, and it's an essential part of your science fair project. Why? The procedure is like a road map. It shows you exactly where you're going and how to get there. It keeps you from getting lost or distracted along the way.

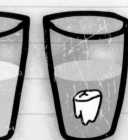

Water   Soda   Sports drink   Juice

Are We There Yet?

Here's how a procedure might look for our tooth experiment.

STEP 1: Set four identical cups next to each other in your experiment area.

STEP 2: Label each cup with the name of one experimental liquid.

STEP 3: Pour identical amounts of the appropriate liquids into each cup.

STEP 4: Let the cups sit for two hours to equalize the liquids' temperatures.

STEP 5: Drop one tooth into each cup.

STEP 6: Leave the cups undisturbed for three days.

STEP 7: Get four see-through plastic bags. Label each bag with the name of one experimental liquid.

STEP 8: Remove the teeth from the cups. Place them immediately into the appropriate plastic bags to avoid mix-ups.

STEP 9: One by one, remove each tooth from its bag. Examine it with a magnifier and record your observations. Return each tooth to its bag before moving on to a new one.

Repeat After Me

Remember way, way back in the beginning of the book, when we said good science experiments needed to be repeatable? The procedure makes this possible. Any decent scientist can follow well-written steps. It's kind of like reading a recipe, only the end result is science instead of, say, a **cherry pie.**

See how easy it is? Come up with a list of steps for your own experiment. Follow the steps to science fair victory.

Take Note: Turn to P. 14 of your logbook. Use this page to record your procedure.

All the Right Stuff

You just learned that a science fair procedure will get you from point A to point B, and **that's great**. But do you know what makes it even better? Your procedure isn't just a road map. It's a shopping list, too.

Yep, it's true. You probably didn't even realize you were **making** a list. But when you figured out your experiment, you also identified the **equipment** and other **stuff** you're going to need. **Pretty cool, right?**

To see how it works, let's look again at the sample procedure on P. 55. After rereading the steps, we realize that we need the following materials:

Step 1:	Four identical cups.
Step 2:	A permanent marker (to label the cups).
Step 3:	Experimental liquids and possibly a measuring cup.
Step 4:	Nothing.
Step 5:	Four teeth.
Step 6:	Nothing.
Step 7:	Four see-through plastic bags, plus the permanent marker again.
Step 8:	Nothing.
Step 9:	A magnifier.

Time to Raid the Piggybank

You've identified your materials. Now you need to figure out how much they'll cost. That's right—you're going to have to shell out actual cash for some of this stuff, or at least convince your parents to do it. **Because science supplies don't grow on trees, ya know.**

Our tooth experiment, luckily, seems to be pretty affordable. We might have to buy a sleeve of plastic cups and some baggies. We can probably find the other stuff around the house. **We're getting off easy here.**

But not all experiments are this cheap. You might need expensive equipment or other supplies for your project. Try to borrow this stuff if you possibly can. (We hear your science teacher is a soft touch.) If borrowing isn't an option, it's time to raid that piggybank. Or you can redesign your experiment to get rid of the pricey stuff. It's your call.

Take Note: Turn to P. 15 of your logbook. Make a shopping list for your project

A Sad Tale

For her science fair project, Emily needed the world's easiest materials: some eggs and a pencil. She wasn't the tiniest bit worried about her shopping. "I'll do it next week," she thought.

But before Emily could get to the store, the Chickens' Union declared a strike. Members wouldn't lay a single egg until their demands were met. Negotiations were expected to continue for weeks.

On the very same day, every store in the world sold out of pencils. No one knows why. It was a freak coincidence.

Emily panicked. She went to every grocery and stationery store in town. But she couldn't find any eggs or pencils. So she was forced to change her experiment. She did a boring, smelly project about Brussels sprouts instead.

The moral of this story is: Don't wait until the last minute to do your shopping. Sure, Emily's tale is a bit far-fetched. But the concept is not. Figure out where you're going to get your supplies, and then do it. It's better to be too early...than too late.

Have I Got a Proposal for You!

You are **seriously** getting your act together, and we're impressed. **Really.** You've slogged through variables and controls and procedures and materials...**phew!** **Anyone can see that you know your stuff.**

They can see it, that is, if you **show** them. And this leads us to a little gem called the **science fair proposal**.

A science fair proposal is a written statement that explains what you plan to do. It's not really important to your experiment. It **may** be important, however, to your teacher or the science fair judges. These people want to make sure that your project isn't shaping up to be a **big fat waste of everyone's time**. A proposal is an easy way to show them you're on the right track.

By this point, the proposal should be a total breeze for you. It includes **five easy parts**, all of which you've already done:

1. **Title.** Your project's title goes at the top of the page.

2. **Problem.** This is the burning question that you intend to answer.

3. **Hypothesis.** State your hypothesis. No extra explanation required.

4. **Materials:** List the materials you came up with on PP. 56 and 57.

5. **Procedure:** List the steps, just like we did on P. 55. **It's that simple.**

Summing It Up

In earlier sections, we covered the individual parts of our tooth experiment. Let's put them together and see what they look like in proposal form.

The Effect of Sugary Drinks on Human Teeth

Problem: Do sugary drinks really rot teeth?

Hypothesis: Sugary drinks will cause human teeth to decay.

Materials: Four identical cups, permanent marker, soda, juice, sports drink, water, measuring cup, four human teeth, four see-through plastic bags, magnifier, logbook.

Procedure: Blah blah blah, steps 1 through 9, too long to repeat. See P. 55 if you need a reminder.

See how easy that was?

It's clear that you really **get** your experiment now. All you need is your teacher's approval to move on to the next stage: actually **doing the project**.

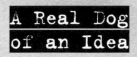

A Real Dog of an Idea

Animal experiments are frowned upon by most science fairs. Are you proposing to shoot Rover into space? See how Goldie reacts to changes in her tank temperature? Test whether Meowzer really does have nine lives? Don't be surprised if your project gets rejected at the proposal stage.

I Want My Mummy

A good experiment has one independent variable, a control, and a simple design. This experiment hits all three points.

The Idea:

Jeremy has been reading about mummies. He knows that the ancient Egyptians used a certain salt as a drying agent. He wonders if any salt would do the job. To find out, he decides to mummify things using different salts.

The Problem:

Jeremy is way into mummies. He'd love to mummify apples, and hot dogs, and dead lizards, and flowers, and anything else he can find. But he's worried about making things too complicated. Also, Jeremy knows that sunlight dries things out. He wonders if it does a better job than salt.

The Solution:

To keep things simple, Jeremy decides to stick to apples. (They're the **coolest** because he can carve faces into them before he mummifies them.) He'll just have one independent variable: the type of salt. For controls, he'll leave one apple in the sunlight and one sitting on the kitchen counter. Jeremy now has a simple but interesting project on his hands.

Things to Think About:

 How will I measure the effect of each salt?

 Why is one salt different from another? Should they have different effects?

➡ How will I make sure the apples I use are as similar as possible?

➡ How long do I think it will take to mummify an apple? What's my project timeline?

➡ Other issues (come up with your own):
_____

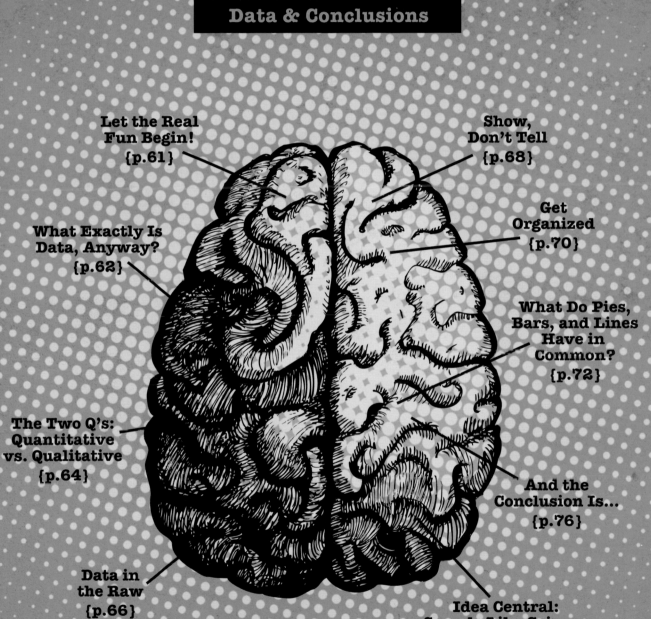

Let the Real
Fun Begin!
{p.61}

Show,
Don't Tell
{p.68}

What Exactly Is
Data, Anyway?
{p.62}

Get
Organized
{p.70}

What Do Pies,
Bars, and Lines
Have in
Common?
{p.72}

The Two Q's:
Quantitative
vs. Qualitative
{p.64}

And the
Conclusion Is...
{p.76}

Data in
the Raw
{p.66}

Idea Central:
Sounds Like Science
{p.78}

Let the Real Fun Begin!

You've done an awful lot of legwork to get to this point. You're probably itching to get your hands on some actual science. And guess what?

The time has come. You're as ready as you'll ever be to:

(drum roll, please)

dive into your experiment.

That means we need to get serious here. In this section, we're going to have a heart-to-heart chat about **data**—what it is, how to get it, what to do with it, and much more. **Feeling hungry?**

Good, because the information **smorgasbord** is about to begin!

What Exactly is Data, Anyway?

Review time! Go back to PP. 46 and 47 for a sec. Reread the information about independent and dependent variables. **Oh, yeah.**

Now you remember.

There's a reason we asked you to refresh your memory. It's because we're about to bring those variables back for an encore. This time, though, we're going to call them something different. We're going to call them **data**.

Data is a scientific word that means information or results. Put even more simply, it just means **things you keep track of**. You're going to **keep track of** the changes you make to your independent variable. You're going to **keep track of** what happens to the dependent variable as a result. The data you gather during this process is the cornerstone of your project.

Let's go back to the squirrels and rotten teeth to see how it works. Here are some facts, i.e., data, that you might record during those experiments.

Squirrel Food Choices

Independent variable:
- Items in a food mixture

Data you might track:
- What foods you include in the mixture
- How many pieces of food you use at one time
- Where you place the food

Dependent variable:
- Which items squirrels choose most

Data you might track:
- Exactly which items are chosen from the mixture
- The order in which the items are chosen
- Any items that are **not** chosen

The Effect of Sugary Liquids on Human Teeth

Independent variable:
- Type of liquid

Data you might track:
- The names of the liquids used
- Amount of liquid used
- Grams of sugar in each liquid (from the drink's nutritional label)

Dependent variable:
- Liquid's effect on teeth

Data you might track:
- Degree of tooth decay*

*Actually, this doesn't even begin to cover it. We'll get into more detail on PP. 66 and 67.

Pieces of the Puzzle

Scientists put many bits of data together to form conclusions. One science fair participant compares the process to doing a puzzle. "The more little pieces you put together, the better you can see the entire picture. I like the feeling of accomplishment I get at the end," she says.

The Two Q's:
Quantitative vs. Qualitative

There's a certain word we avoided when we defined "data" on PP. 62 and 63. Now, though, it's time to face that sucker head-on.

The word is: numbers.

See how we put the word in **great big, bold letters**? We did that so you can't possibly miss it. **Yes, it's that important.**

Numbers are **absolutely essential** in a good science fair project. Specifically, we're talking about **data that can be recorded as numbers**. How many? How long? How big? How fast? All of these questions can be answered in number form.

But here's the big pitfall. The questions we asked in the last paragraph can be answered **without** numbers, too. **Check it out.**

	With numbers	Without numbers
How many?	17	A lot
How long?	8 hours, 20 minutes	All day
How big?	5 cm	Shortest
How fast?	10 kilometers per hour	A fast run

Data that uses numbers is called **quantitative data**. Data that doesn't use numbers is called **qualitative data**. **Quantitative data is almost always better than qualitative data.** So, find ways to use numbers whenever you possibly can.

Sinking Our Teeth into Some Numbers

Let's get back to the tooth experiment for a minute. Imagine you're ready to examine your sugar-soaked teeth. You peer through your magnifier and see that the soda tooth is way more decayed than the other three.

So, here's your problem. You can see the decay. But you can't just say, "This tooth is more rotten than the other ones." You need numbers to back up your observations.

This is where you have to get creative. What can you count or measure? Maybe you could count decay pits on each tooth. Maybe you could weigh the teeth before and after soaking to see what percentage of mass they lose. Maybe you could measure the teeth to see if they have shrunk, and if so, how much. Just to hammer the point home, **examine these two statements:**

"The soda tooth decayed the most."

vs.

"The soda tooth lost the greatest percentage of its original mass."

The statement with the quantitative data is a bit more convincing, don'tcha think? Yeah, we think so, too. **And the science fair judges will agree—guaranteed.**

THINK METRIC

Did you notice that we used metric measurements in our examples? That's because the metric system is standard for scientists everywhere. Join the club! Go metric in your project. Ask your teacher or a parent for help if you're not quite sure how it works.

Helpful Hint
Some good science fair projects have qualitative elements. If you're in this boat, don't panic. But do talk to your science teacher. He or she can tell you if your approach is okay.

Data in the Raw

Independent variables…dependent variables…quantitative data… keeping track of it all. Are you getting the impression that you're going to have a whole pile of facts to deal with pretty soon?

If so, you're absolutely right!

Science experiments can generate **oodles** of data. **Barrels** of it. **Oceans** of it. Which means that depending on your experiment, you might end up **swimming in the stuff**.

This initial flash flood of information is called **raw data**. It gets this name because it's just a bunch of untouched—that is to say, **raw**—facts. You haven't thought about the data yet, or organized it in any way, or drawn any conclusions about it. **You'll do that later.** For now, your job is to keep those facts coming—**and to record them every step of the way.**

On the Record

Your science fair logbook is the perfect place to record raw data. Jot notes as you do your experiment. **(Date and time? What drink did I use? How much of it? How many grams of sugar?)** It's fine to include both qualitative and quantitative data at this point.

Two key points about this:

Do it now. Record data as it occurs. **Always.** You might think you'll remember how much Super Slushie Sugar Buster you poured into Cup A. But what if the phone rings and distracts you? **Oops. You forgot.** Don't let this happen to you. **Write it down now**.

Do it in pen. Always use a pen to record raw data. Pen marks can't be erased. This means they can't be changed or faked. (Although YOU would never do that, right?) Make a mistake when you're entering data? **No problem.** Just cross it out and start again.

MORE IS BETTER

When it comes to raw data, more is almost always better. Think about it. If an experiment works once, **that's interesting**. If it works five times in a row, **you're clearly onto something**. If it works ten times in a row, well, **that's very darn impressive**. You can be almost sure that your results are valid.

Think about ways to build multiple trials into your science fair project. You'll probably do better in the judging if you do. You'll learn more about your topic, too.

Take Note: Turn to PP. 16–19 of your logbook. Use these pages to record raw data.

Show, Don't Tell

There's an old saying: **A picture is worth a thousand words.** This means it's easier to understand things you can see. Think about it. What gives you a better mental image: an hour-long description of a cute puppy, or an actual photo of the little furball? **Well, duh.**

The picture, of course.

You can take advantage of this fact. Keep your camera handy as you crank up your experiment. Take pictures of **anything** and **everything** you think might be useful later. **Go snap-happy!**

Helpful Hint

Your camera probably has a lot of cool features, like a close-up mode or red-eye reduction. **Learn how to use these features.** They can help you to take better pictures. Better pictures give you a more eye-catching display. They might even land you a higher score on your project.

Photo Ops

Here are some things you might consider photographing:

Your work area. You went to a lot of effort with your setup. Why not show it off? Ask a friend to take the snapshot so you can be in the picture, if you like. **Say cheese!**

Experiment sites. Your project may take you interesting places. For example, you might visit a park to feed squirrels. Pictures of your experiment sites let the judges "see" through your eyes.

Equipment. Big and bulky equipment probably shouldn't go to the science fair. Photograph this stuff instead.

Banned stuff. Bacteria, flames, lasers, animals. They're cool, but you can't take 'em to the fair. Photograph these and other items on the "don't-bring" list instead.

Changes over time. Photos are a great way to log plant growth, tooth decay, fungus infestations, color changes, or other results with a visual **"Wow"** factor.

Why Here? Why Now?

Let's pause for a quickie clarification before we move on. You might think a photography discussion doesn't belong in the middle of our data section. **After all, photos aren't data.**

True. But they do **supplement** your data. They make it easier to understand, which is always a good thing.

So, take and display those pictures with pride!

DID YOU KNOW?

The objects in a photograph are called **subjects**. The placement of the subjects is called the **composition**.

Get Organized

Time warp! We just skipped a few days or weeks of your life. We've jumped to the moment when you wipe the sweat from your brow and heave a sigh of relief. That's right—your experiment is **done. History. Finito.**

Your work, however, is not. Remember that **ocean of data** we talked about a few pages ago? You're swimming in it. And you need to get organized, **pronto**, if you want to avoid drowning.

So, let's hop to it! The first thing you need to do is make something called a **data table**, or a **table** for short. A table is a grid that pulls all your data together in one place. It sorts the data into rows and columns. This arrangement helps you to see patterns in your information.

Scientist's Choice

Take a closer look at the tables on this page. Do you think some data is missing? Like, for instance, we didn't put dates on the tooth table. We also didn't record our total squirrel sightings for our squirrel experiment.

That's right. We didn't. We didn't think those things affected our outcome. So, we didn't bother with them.

But that's just us. If **you** were doing these experiments, you might have a different opinion. **And that's okay.** There is no right or wrong way to make a table. Include whatever information **floats your boat.** You'll cross that ocean with no trouble at all.

Sample Tables

The easiest way to understand tables is to look at them. Here's how data tables might look for our squirrel and tooth experiments.

Squirrel Food Choices

Date	Location	Duration	Nuts taken	Berries taken	Seeds taken	Taken first?
April 15	Home	30 minutes	7	2	4	Berry
April 16	Park	30 minutes	5	1	4	Seed
April 17	Woods	30 minutes	6	1	2	Nut
April 18	Lake	30 minutes	6	0	3	Nut
April 19	Field	30 minutes	4	2	3	Nut

The Effect of Sugary Liquids on Human Teeth

Substance	Duration	Quantity	Sugar (g)	% mass lost*			
				Day 0	Day 1	Day 2	Day 3
Water	3 days	120 ml	0	0	0	0	0
Juice	3 days	120 ml	7	0	0.25	0.5	1
Sports drink	3 days	120 ml	14	0	2	5	9
Soda	3 days	120 ml	15	0	3	7	11

* We're imagining that we weighed the teeth every day during the course of our experiment. Just go with us on this one. You'll see why in a few pages.

See how well that works? You magically transformed your data from **scribble-scrabble** to a **model of scientific organization**.

Nice work, scientist!

Disclaimer: We made up this data, so it's probably wrong. Don't even THINK about using it as a resource.

Helpful Hint
You can draw tables by hand, if you like. But most students find it easier to create them on the computer. Programs called spreadsheets organize any type of data in table form. Ask a grownup to show you how to do it.

Take Note: Turn to P. 20 of your logbook. Insert your data into the blank grid.

What Do Pies, Bars, and Lines Have in Common?

You've assembled your data in an easy-to-read format. And you're starting to see patterns. No, not **plaid** or **stripes** or **polka dots**. We're talking about **information patterns** here.

Look back at the tables on P. 71. What patterns pop out at you? Well, for starters, you can see that squirrels chose nuts first (or: before berries or seeds) three out of five times. You can also see that some teeth were much more affected by their three-day soak than others. And you'll probably notice a bunch of other stuff if you spend more time looking. **Your results are starting to emerge.**

Now it's time to coax those results out into the open. You're going to do this by turning your data into pictures that anyone can understand at a glance. Those pictures are called **graphs**.

What's Your Type?

There are three main types of graphs: **pie charts**, **bar graphs**, and **line graphs**. These graphs have different uses. Let's look at each type and see how it might work for you.

```
Helpful Hint
Many word-processing programs can draw
charts. Learn to use this feature. It
will make your job much, much easier.
```

The Pie Chart

It's not hard to see where the pie chart got its name.

These charts are round and divided into wedges, like pies. Use a pie chart when you need to chop a total amount of something—**anything**—into segments.

Want Some Pie?

Some of our squirrel data will work as a pie chart. The squirrels took a certain amount of food. That's our **total**. Within that total, the squirrels took several different types of food. Those are our **wedges**.

Here's how the data looks in pie chart form.

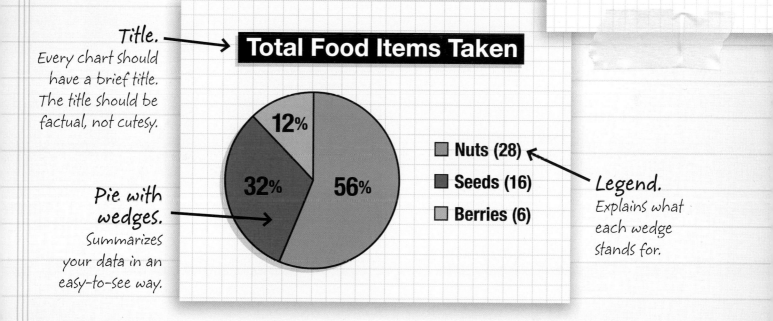

Title.
Every chart should have a brief title. The title should be factual, not cutesy.

Total Food Items Taken

12%

32% 56%

☐ Nuts (28)
☐ Seeds (16)
☐ Berries (6)

Legend.
Explains what each wedge stands for.

Pie with wedges.
Summarizes your data in an easy-to-see way.

Have Some More Pie, Dear

Need more examples?

These results would all work as pie charts.

● Favorite colors of the students in a classroom
● Results (1, 2, 3, 4, 5, or 6) of 100 die tosses
● Total weeds in your yard divided by type

The Bar Graph

Now we're really going to raise the bar—the **bar graph**, that is! Bar graphs look like, you guessed it, a bunch of bars. They are very handy tools. Use them when you need to show differences in frequency, amount, or some other quantity.

The Best, Bar None

A bar graph will really show off some of the tooth data. Our four teeth lost different percentages of their mass. We can easily put those numbers into bar form. Let's see how it looks.

Just the Facts About Bar Graphs

○ A bar graph compares quantities.

○ Each bar represents a certain quantity. Taller bars show larger quantities.

○ **Quantities** to be compared are listed along the vertical (up-and-down) axis.

○ **Items** to be compared are listed along the horizontal (side-to-side) axis.

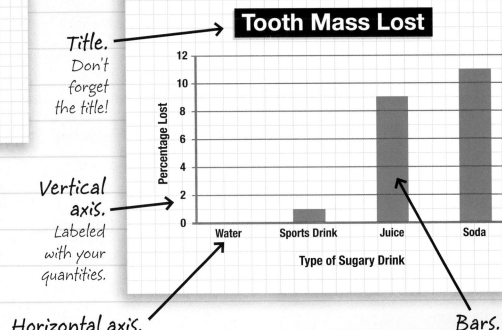

Title. Don't forget the title!

Vertical axis. Labeled with your quantities.

Horizontal axis. Labeled with your items.

Bars. The height of each bar rises to show the appropriate quantity.

Tooth Mass Lost

Percentage Lost

Type of Sugary Drink

Water   Sports Drink   Juice   Soda

```
Step Up to the Science Bar
Not quite clear yet?
Here are some more results that work as bar graphs.
● Top speed of a model car using different lubricants
● Height of bean plants grown under different conditions
● Length of time different cereals stay crisp in milk
```

The Line Graph

Are you dying to know about the third type of graph? Well, get in line! **Line graphs** are similar in format to bar graphs, but they have jagged lines instead of solid bars. Use them when you need to show changes or trends over time.

The Line Starts Here

Let's say we want to get fancy with our tooth data. We want to show how the teeth changed over time. With a line graph, we can do that. Here's how it looks.

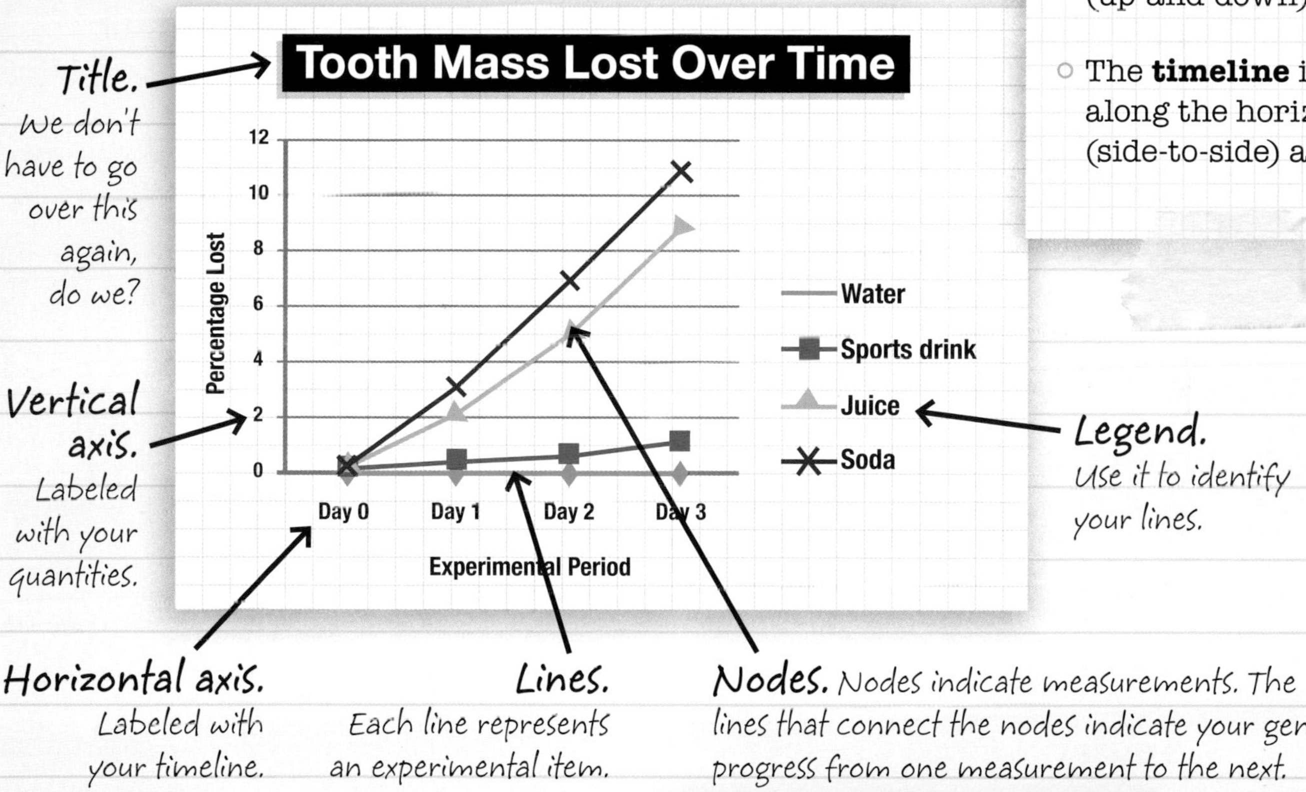

Just the Facts About Line Graphs

- A line graph shows changes over time.

- Each line represents one experimental item.

- **Quantities** to be compared are listed along the vertical (up-and-down) axis.

- The **timeline** is listed along the horizontal (side-to-side) axis.

Title. *We don't have to go over this again, do we?*

Tooth Mass Lost Over Time

Percentage Lost

12
10
8
6
4
2
0

Day 0   Day 1   Day 2   Day 3

Experimental Period

Water
Sports drink
Juice
Soda

Vertical axis. *Labeled with your quantities.*

Legend. *Use it to identify your lines.*

Horizontal axis. *Labeled with your timeline.*

Lines. *Each line represents an experimental item.*

Nodes. *Nodes indicate measurements. The lines that connect the nodes indicate your general progress from one measurement to the next.*

Toe the Line

Looking for a little more info? These results would work as line graphs.

- The progress of different substances dissolving in water
- Growth rates of different vegetables
- Increases in fitness level over a two-week period

Turn to P. 21 of your logbook. Use the templates to start your own bar and line graphs.

Take Note:

And the Conclusion Is

That graphing stuff was tough, wasn't it? **But it was worth it.** You can now see exactly where you stand with your data. And that means you're ready to take the last giant step of the experimental process. You're ready to draw a **conclusion**.

In one way, a conclusion is a simple thing. It's just a statement that says whether your hypothesis was right or wrong. **Easy.** But in another way, the conclusion is a **towering milestone**. It's the answer you've been seeking all this time. Pretty cool, eh?

So, Where Do I Start?

Even though your conclusion is important, there's nothing tricky about writing it. Start by rereading your hypothesis. Look at your tables and your graphs. Decide what you think the data shows. Then, write a few sentences explaining whether your hypothesis was right or wrong. **Alakazam! You have your conclusion.**

To illustrate the point, let's check in with our squirrels and teeth.

Squirrel Food Choices

Hypothesis: Squirrels will choose nuts more often than any other food.

Conclusion: Five trials were conducted in different areas, on different days, with different squirrels. Squirrels in all five areas took more nuts than other foods. This data supports the hypothesis. Squirrels do choose nuts more often than any other food.

The Effect of Sugary Drinks on Human Teeth

Hypothesis: Sugary drinks will cause human teeth to decay.

Conclusion: Human teeth placed in sugary drinks showed clear signs of decay. The effect was greatest in the drinks with the highest sugar content. Teeth placed in drinks without sugar did not decay. This data supports the hypothesis. Sugary drinks do cause human teeth to decay.

Simple stuff, right? But you can see that it gets the job done. You did the work, you crunched the numbers, and now you get to show off the results. **Be proud, scientist.** We know **we** are. In fact, we're getting a little choked up here. ***Sniff.*** Hankie, please!

By the Numbers

A few points to remember about your conclusion:

 It must be based solely on the numbers in your logbook. Your opinions and observations don't count, bud.

 If you can't reach a conclusion based on your numbers, we have bad news: You're not done. Do a few more trials to generate more data.

 We said this before, but we'll say it again. Don't worry if your hypothesis is wrong. Say it loud, say it proud. Just say it...in your conclusion.

Sounds Like Science

Some experiments are easier to graph than others. Here's one that will work perfectly as a bar graph.

The Idea:

Nikki's mom is a musician. She has a lot of cool musical equipment. Nikki thinks she'll take advantage of this resource. She decides to make a xylophone by filling drinking glasses with water, then "playing" them with spoons. She'll use her mom's guitar tuner to adjust the xylophone's pitch.

The Problem:

Nikki needs to turn her invention into an investigation. And she really wants to chart her results.

The Solution:

Nikki realizes that she has never heard of a lemonade xylophone, or a vinegar xylophone, or a milk xylophone. She wonders if these liquids would work, and if they would affect the glasses' pitch. She thinks it would be fun to investigate this question. She also thinks the results would look great in a bar graph. A bar graph even kind of looks like a xylophone, which is supercool! Nikki will use "xylophony" colors when she makes her graphics.

Things to Think About:

➡ Will temperature affect the glasses' pitch? How can I control for this?

➡ Will carbonated liquids act differently than non-carbonated ones?

➡ I'll need a lot of identical glasses. Where can I buy them cheaply?

➡ My liquid measurements need to be very precise. How will I handle this?

➡ Other issues (come up with your own)
_____

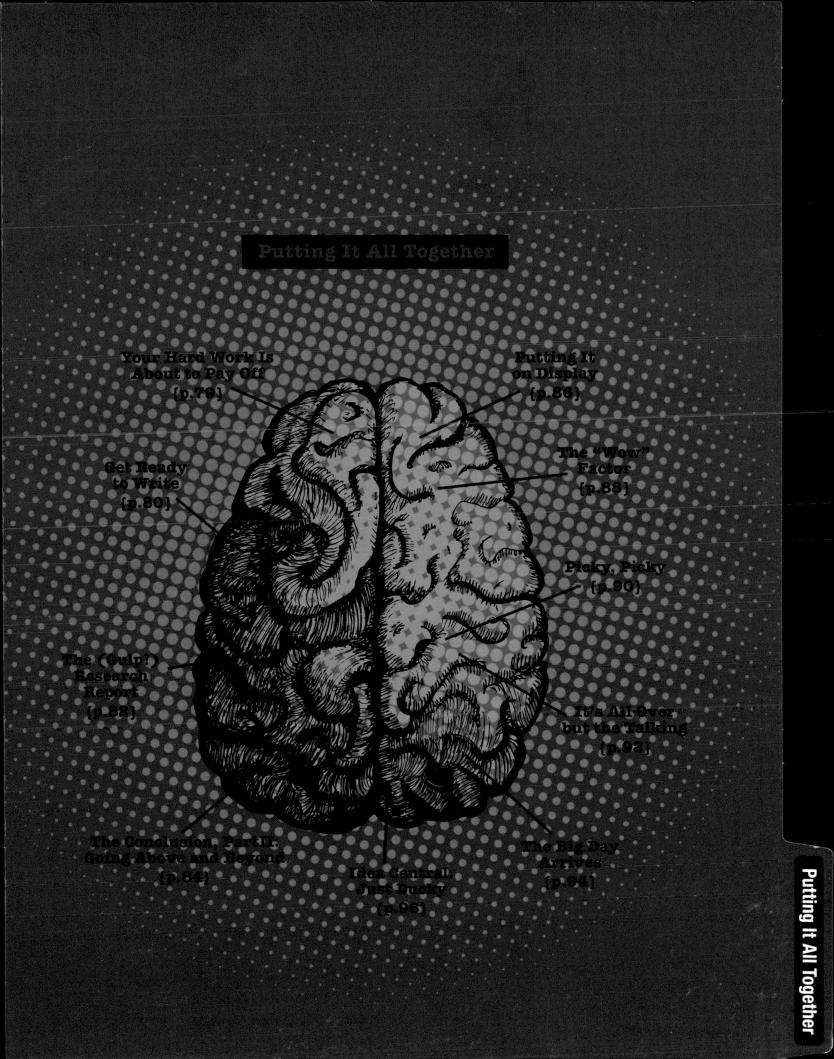

Putting It All Together

Your Hard Work Is
About to Pay Off
{p.78}

Get Ready
to Write
{p.80}

The (Gulp!)
Research
Report
{p.82}

The Conclusion, Part II:
Going Above and Beyond
{p.84}

Idea Central:
Just Ducky
{p.96}

Putting It
on Display
{p.86}

The "Wow"
Factor
{p.88}

Picky, Picky
{p.90}

It's All Over
but the Talking
{p.92}

The Big Day
Arrives
{p.94}

Your Hard Work is About to Pay Off

You have worked so hard, scientist! Wouldn't it be great if people could peer directly into your brain—like, maybe through your **left ear**—and see everything you've learned? They can't, though. So, it's time to show them. And the best place to do that is, you guessed it, at a **real, live science fair**.

You have a few things to do before you can take this big step. You still have to write a report and make a display. You need to be ready to talk about your project, too. **Gulp!** Scary stuff, right? But don't worry. **You can pull it all together—and we can show you how**.

Let's get **prepared** for the fair!

Get Ready to Write

Can you feel the knowledge flowing through your veins? You're practically **bursting** with the stuff. That's a good thing, because you're going to write down everything you know in a paper called a **research report**.

If you've done your work (and we know you have), the research report should be pretty easy. Don't let it scare you. But don't underestimate it, either. Take your report seriously, and spend a little time organizing before you sit down to write. **You'll be glad you did.**

Time for Miracles

On P. 39, we called index cards little organizational miracles. You have now arrived at the miracle moment! Lay your cards on a table. Move them around to put your notes in different orders. Find the order that makes perfect sense. Ta-da! Outline done!

Before You Begin

These simple steps will get you ready to write.

Gather your references. Remember all those notes you took at the beginning of your project? Well, **they're about to come in handy.** Gather your photocopies, notes, logbook, and index cards. Take a trip to the library, if necessary, to re-borrow your reference books. You'll want as much information as possible at your fingertips.

Review your references. It's been a while since you did your research. You probably need a little memory booster. So, reread your notes. If they don't give you enough information, reread your original references. We hate to say "I told you so," but remember when we talked about taking good notes? Yeah, **we told you so.**

Evaluate your information. You've reviewed your research. Now you have to figure out what's important. Does a reader need to understand squirrels' feeding habits? The process of tooth decay? Decide which facts are absolute "musts" for your research report, and dump any that aren't. **Be merciless.** You're looking for the nuts and bolts here.

Make an outline. You don't have to outline your data or your hypothesis. But it will help you **a lot** to outline your background information. The outline doesn't have to be fancy. Just jot your facts in a logical order. You'll follow this outline when the time comes to write your report.

Take Note: Turn to PP. 22 and 23 of your logbook. Use these pages to outline your background information.

The (Gulp!) Research Report

So, you have organized and reviewed until you're blue in the face. You're pretty sure you haven't missed a single, solitary fact. Which means you can't put it off any longer. You're as ready as you'll ever be to actually **write** your research report.

We aren't going to lie to you. The body of your research report will require some deep thinking. The format, however, will not. There's a tried-and-true way of tackling these things. Here are the parts you should include in your report.

Working in Reverse

Sometimes it's easiest to write from back to front. Start with the bibliography. Work your way backward to the abstract, which can be tricky to write.

Research Report Basics

Title page. The first page of your report is like a cover. It includes your experiment's title plus your name, your class or school, and the date.

Summary sheet. The summary sheet highlights the "bare bones" of your project. It's a single page that includes your proposal (which we went over on PP. 58-59), plus your results and your conclusion.

Abstract. This is where the actual writing begins. The abstract is a short summary of your project. Your goal is to explain your purpose, procedure, and conclusion in a few paragraphs. This might be the only part of your report that the judges actually read. So, **make it good**!

Research Report Basics-cont'd

Introduction and background. This section gives readers any background information they need in order to understand your experiment. All that stuff you learned about squirrels and teeth? This is where you stick it.

Methods. This is where you explain your experiment—in agonizing detail. Think of it as an instruction manual. After reading this section, anyone should be able to copy your work. (**And that's okay.** Remember, in science, copying can be good.)

Results. Explain what you learned. This section will include your data tables, charts, graphs, and possibly some photographs. This is also where you would come clean if you **goofed anything up**.

Conclusion. This is your big moment! You get to tell the world whether your hypothesis was right or wrong, and why.*

Bibliography. Sometimes also called "References." Other scientists (and, more importantly, your teacher) want to know where you got your information. This section identifies the books, articles, websites, and other resources you used during your research.

Helpful Hint

Never hand-write a research report. Your paper needs to look tidy, which means it needs to be done on a computer. So, learn how to use a word processing program and a printer. If you don't have these tools at home, borrow them. Most public libraries offer free computer access. Your school probably has computers you can use, too.

Make It Work for You

Not all research reports follow the format we just described. Your teacher might want something slightly different. Or you might want to tweak things to suit your project better. **That's fine.** Feel free to change things up. Just make sure you're getting your message across.

As long as you do that, you can consider your report a success.

*We'll gab more about this on PP. 84-85.

The Conclusion, Part II: Going Above and Beyond

Did you see that little **asterisk-thingy on the bottom of P. 83? Fantastic!** Then you already know what we're going to talk about next. We're going to get a bit more detailed about your conclusion section.

Or rather, we're going to help **you** get a bit more detailed. **Here's the thing:** The conclusion doesn't have to end after you discuss your hypothesis. **You can take it further.** And let us tell you, judges **love** it when students do that. They **eat it right up.** Which means high scores, blue ribbons, fame, fortune, **confetti falling from the ceiling**, and so on.

So, you want to go for the glory.

There are three classic ways to get it.

See You Next Year!

A really good conclusion section can be a goldmine for your science fair career. Did you figure out how to make your experiment better? Great! Do the new-and-improved version for next year's fair. Found a great new direction? Ditto. Next year, springboard off those ideas for future fairs. You may never need to brainstorm a brand-spanking-new idea again!

Add these topics to your conclusion section:

Improvements. You learned a lot during your experiment. And maybe, just maybe, you're kicking yourself now. You wish you had done things differently. Well, here's your chance to say so. Go into detail about ways to make your experiment better, or easier, or more practical, or whatever. Don't worry; you won't make yourself look bad. On the contrary, you'll show your **personal growth**.

New directions. Maybe your experiment gave you an idea for **another** experiment. The new project might continue your current work. Or it might tackle a related problem. Whatever the idea is, **mention it**. The judges will see that your brain is working. And that's what you want, right?

Applications. This is science fair speak for "What good is my project, anyway?" Point out some real-world uses, i.e. applications, of your research. Like, maybe you think it would be a good idea to install nut dispensers in parks for those snackin' squirrels. Or you'd like to require dental education for all soda drinkers. Share your ideas...make the world a better place...and win prizes at the same time. **How great is that??**

MAKING AN IMPACT

The **applications** section can be the most interesting part of your project. "There are many problems that need solutions or things that could be improved to make our world a better place. I think it's great that through science, anyone with an idea can make a big impact on the Earth and human life," says one science fair participant.

Putting It on Display

Ready to stop **experimenting** and start **creating**? That's right. We're finally ready to talk about the science fair **display**.

The display is the setup you'll use on fair day. It sums up your work through words, pictures, graphs, and props. Most people will just glance at your display. A few really curious ones (like your teacher, and the judges, and your **proud Nana**) will probably take a closer look. Your display needs to work for both casual and serious lookers.

A three-panel **backboard** is a good way to get the job done. If you're lucky, your school might have a pile of these things that students can borrow. If not, you might have to make your own. Foam-core board, cardboard, and wood are typical building materials.

There's no one-size-fits-all, set-in-stone standard for backboards. Check to see if your science fair requires any specific measurements or formats. If not, **go for it—get creative!**

Under Cover

Many students cover their backboards with felt for a finished look. You can buy big sheets of felt at fabric stores (or, actually, at any store that sells fabric on rolls). Stretch the felt tightly over your board. Then, staple it in place.

Think about these things before whipping out the hammer and duct tape!

Space. You'll only get a small bit of space at the science fair. You can't fit a super-sized display into a kiddie-meal spot.

Travel. You have to lug your display to the fair. Don't make it too awkward or heavy to carry.

Gravity. Your display has to stand up by itself. Make sure it passes the no-flop test.

HELPFUL HINT

Judges will read your layout like a book, from top left to bottom right. Make sure it follows a logical flow.

What to Say, What to Say?

Let's assume you've figured out the mechanics of your backboard.

Now you're wondering what to do with the darn thing.

Luckily for you, this part is pretty straightforward. You're going to recreate your research report on the backboard. You can use the short parts (like the hypothesis) as-is. You'll summarize the longer ones (like your background research) to fit into a smaller area. You'll arrange all of the parts in a layout that really **shows off your stuff**.

Purpose	Title		Results
Hypothesis	Tables	Graphs	Conclusion
Background	Photos		Applications/ Future Studies
Methods	Data Discussion		Bibliography

Here's a layout that has worked for many students. Mess with it as necessary to suit your project.

87

The "Wow" Factor

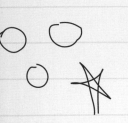

First and foremost, your display gives information. **That's Job #1 here.** But how can you communicate if no one is paying attention? The simple answer is: **you can't.** And that's why your display has a **secondary** purpose: It must attract attention. You could say it needs the **"Wow"** factor.

The **"Wow"** factor is more about looks than substance. It's about making your project stand out from the crowd. About convincing people to glance **your** way a second or third time. Maybe even **(dare we dream?)** making them **stop** at your spot and ask a few questions.

Helpful Hint

To plan your display, lay your backboard on the floor. Set your presentation pieces (title cards, photos, graphs, etc.) on the backboard. Move the pieces around until you find an arrangement you like.

Letters at Large

You'll need **BIG** letters for your display title. You have four ways to get them.

Buy them. Art supply stores sell alphabet cutouts. Choose the size and color you need.

Print them. Your home computer can create and print big letters.

Make them. Cut out your own construction-paper letters.

Draw them. Write or paint directly on your display. (For art experts only!)

There are countless ways to add visual punch to your project. Here are a few that apply to every project:

`K.I.S.S.` Remember this one? We'll repeat ourselves, just in case: Keep It Simple, Scientist. A jam-packed display may look impressive. But it's also intimidating. Keep things uncluttered to attract more readers.

`LABELS.` Good labels are part of the K.I.S.S. concept. They help people to understand your layout, which makes them more likely to really **look** at it.

`PRETTY COLORS.` There's a reason black-and-white TV died out when the color version came along: It's boring. Black-and-white science fair displays are boring, too. An attractive color scheme will give you the visual boost you need.

`VISIBILITY.` This goes hand-in-hand with the color thing. Make your headlines visible by choosing colors that really "pop" against each other. It might be hard to read yellow letters on a tan background. But hot pink on green? **Now** you're talking!

`INTERESTING PHOTOS.` Most people won't stop to read your abstract. But they **will** stop to look at cool pictures. Showcase your best photos on your display.

`PROPS.` Did you use or create something cool during the course of your experiment? Is it transportable? **Two "Yesses" = Bring it along**. Nothing grabs attention like a nifty gadget!

Picky, Picky

You've finished your display, and it looks great. We're admiring it in our imagination right now. Look at those crisp titles! Those striking colors! Those…um…glue blobs? And **typos**? And **grammatical errors**? **OH, NO!**

Okay, we admit it. We're being dramatic here. But we're trying to make a serious point. It's this: **Little things count.** Yes, you did a lot of work. Yes, maybe that work should speak for itself. **But that's not always the case.** On science fair day, your presentation gets a say, too.

⭐ First Impressions

Why is your presentation so important? It's mostly about first impressions. A messy display makes a bad first impression. So does a poorly written, spelling-challenged research report. Judges may see these things as reflections of your character. In other words: **They might think you're a sloppy worker, period.** Which means they won't trust your project—**or** your results.

You need to avoid this perception at all costs. **It's not hard to do.**

LOOKIN' GOOD

In a recent article, a former science fair judge admitted that appearances do matter. "No doubt about it—a science fair project that **looks** impressive tends to sway the judges," he says.

Just focus on the "Big Three" of project pickiness:

1 **Neatness.** Your research report needs to look nice and tidy. So does your display. This means NO glue blobs. NO ripped felt. NO loose staples. NO clumsy lettering. NO crooked pictures. If any part of your display appears messy, fix it before science fair day.

DID YOU KNOW?

You don't get a second chance to make a first impression!

2 **Spelling.** There's really no excuse for bad spelling. Your word processor's built-in spell checker will catch most errors. Your friends and family can get the rest of them. Ask at least two trusted people to proofread your paper **and** the lettering on your display.

3 **Grammar.** Grammar is tougher than spelling. But **you can conquer it**. Run your work through a grammar checking program. Ask again for that proofreading help. You might also try reading your work out loud. It's easier to hear mistakes that way.

One Exception

Your logbook is one notable exception to the neatness rule. Scribbles, cross-outs, grease stains, **that fly you squashed the other day**—it's all okay. In fact, it's more than okay. These things are evidence that you've been working hard for a long time. So, that three-month-old spaghetti blotch on P. 17? **Fuhgeddaboudit.** Show your messy logbook with pride!

It's All Over but the Talking

Thought you were done, didn't you? But no. You have one more thing to do, and it's an important one. **You have to get ready to gab about your project.** Why? Because on science fair day, the judges won't just **look** at that pretty display you made. They'll want to **hear** about it, too.

The talking part of your project is called the **oral presentation**. **That's kind of a scary term, isn't it?** But it doesn't need to be. The oral presentation is really just a few minutes of **science chit-chat**. You're going to tell the judges about your experiment. They're going to smile and nod and ask a few questions that you know exactly how to answer. It's **child's play**, really.

Still, it's a part of your project, and you need to take it seriously.

So, okay. Let's get serious.

Here are the parts of a good oral presentation.

☐ **Introduction.** Introduce yourself. Tell the judges your name, your age and grade, your school (if necessary), and the title of your experiment.

☐ **Background information.** Sum up your background information. Remember, you're the expert at this point. The judges don't know nearly as much about your topic as you do.

Helpful Hint: Oral presentations are usually about five minutes long. Check to see if your fair has any special time limits or other guidelines.

Methods. Explain how you did your experiment. You don't need to go into all the gory details here. Just give the big picture.

Results and conclusion. Tell the judges what kinds of results you got and what you concluded based on your data. Again, shoot for the big picture. Your goal is to provide an overview, not to flood the judges with every scrap of information you gathered.

Question-and-answer. When you're done talking, the judges will probably ask you a few questions. **This is not a quiz, and they're not trying to stump you.** They are truly curious about your work. If you can't answer a question, admit it. Tell the judges you'll find out—and then **do it**. **Big, big brownie points for you!**

Don't Worry, Be Happy

Compared to the rest of your project, the oral presentation is a cinch. **Truly.** But there's no denying that it's different from everything else you've done. It involves public speaking, and quick thinking, and a LOT of self-confidence. These things make some people very, very nervous.

It's understandable if you feel this way. Just remember, though, that you're not alone. Other students are anxious, too. So, **get a grip on yourself** and **tough it out**. It's all in the name of science!

Helpful Hint: Practice your oral presentation on your friends and family members. Let them ask questions when you're done. You'll see right away if there are any holes in your knowledge. Correct these problems before science fair day arrives.

The Big Day Arrives

Wow, check this out. There's only one more page left in this entire book. **There it is.**

We're almost out of space, and you know what that means. It means you're almost done. No more reading or prep work or **anything**. Except packing, of course. You have to get your stuff ready to take to the fair. But that's **totally easy**. A big tote bag, a cardboard box or two, and you're ready to rock and roll. So, go ahead and **shout it out:**

We always knew you could do it. Way to go!

"My science fair project is DONE!"

Be Prepared

So, tomorrow, you head to the fair. You can handle this in one of two ways.

| You can run around like a frantic, headless chicken in the morning, packing up your display and anything else you need. | **or** | You can take your time and do it tonight. Then, you can get a good night's sleep. Tomorrow, you can enjoy a hot shower and a relaxed breakfast before leaving the house. |

Hmmmm. The decision isn't too tough when you put it that way, is it? What we're saying here is **don't wait until the last minute to get your act together.** Gather your supplies now to prevent last-minute mistakes and panic attacks.

You're a Winner Already

Being prepared will take some of those butterflies out of your tummy. But it might not zap all of them. You may still be nervous about setting up your display or talking to the judges. Or maybe you just have a bad case of pre-competition jitters. You have your heart set on winning a ribbon. You're worried it won't happen.

You know what? Maybe it will. Maybe it won't. Either way, **it's okay**. You did the work; you did your best; and you learned a LOT. You're a winner no matter what the judges say. And **that** is what the science fair is all about.

Here's Looking at You, Kid

Judges can't help noticing **you the person**, not just **you the scientist**. They'll pay more attention to you—**and your work**—if you present yourself well. **Here's how to do it.**

- Feel well-rested and well-fed • Take a shower and brush your teeth (duh)
- Dress nicely • Shake hands when introduced
- Make eye contact • **Smile** • Speak politely and confidently
- Use appropriate hand gestures while talking • **Listen attentively**

You've known this stuff since you were five years old. It's basic good behavior. At the science fair, however, it's more than that. It's **award-winning** behavior as well.

Take Note: Turn to P. 24 of your logbook. Use the pre-fair checklist to help you get packed.

5

Just Ducky

Some projects have fantastic display potential from Day One. Here's a good example.

The Idea:

Chen lives near a river. The river does not always move at the same speed. Chen would like to monitor the water's flow. He hopes to link the river's speed to environmental conditions, such as rain or drought.

The Problem:

Chen is concerned that his project won't stand out at the science fair. Rivers are brown and boring!

The Solution:

Chen decides to add a visual element to his project. He'll use rubber duckies to track the river's speed. To do this, he'll chuck his plastic pals into the water and time how long it takes them to travel a certain distance. He'll get all the hard information he needs, and he can go totally **quackers** on his display.

Things to Think About:

➡ Should I use the same duckie for every trial? Can I get away with using several styles for better visual impact?

➡ Can I really release the ducks, catch them, and time them, all by myself? Do I need a helper?

➡ I can't really plan my trials. I'll have to wait for rain and other conditions to occur. This might take a long time.

➡ Other issues (come up with your own)
_____